My Sporting Heroes

Jason Mohammad

Published by Accent Press Ltd 2015

ISBN 9781783759361

Printed and bound in the UK

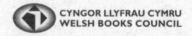

CYNGOR LLYFRAU CYMRU
WELSH BOOKS COUNCIL

Noddir gan
Lywodraeth Cymru
Sponsored by
Welsh Government

This book is dedicated to my three children Lili, Max and Poppy who sometimes have to go weeks on end without seeing their dad. I miss you all and thank you for being the World's Best Children. You have made me very proud.

INTRODUCTION

A FEW YEARS ago I spent a lovely afternoon in the sun with my little boy Max. It was a hot day. I really should have been happy after such a miserable winter. For months, cold and snow had made us dream of the sunshine. It was the coldest winter I can remember. Trust me – sports reporting looks like a glamorous job but standing or sitting in a football stadium can be a very cold experience. I froze doing my Saturday reports for *Final Score*. Anyway – this was a summer to look forward to. But sport – don't you just love it? Sport had ruined it.

Sun shining. Shorts on. Sun cream on. Kicking a ball in the park. Summer was here and yet I just couldn't enjoy it. It was the day after Cardiff City's Premier League dream had died at Wembley and I was left feeling like when the love of your life tells you that 'it's just not working.'

Twenty-four hours after Blackpool had beaten City 3-2, and Brett Ormerod's toe poke had spoiled the capital's hopes of getting back to somewhere near respectability, I still couldn't get that sick feeling out of my stomach. There was no-one in my local park when I went there with the kids on this beautiful summer's day. It was deserted. No kids kicking a ball around pretending to take on Luis Suarez and Wayne Rooney. Not now. Not after *that Saturday*. It could have been so different. My phone didn't ring all day. I couldn't look at the papers. It was just too much. You know you want to cry but you can't. Why does sport do this to us? The shoulders are hunched. The tissues are on standby.

That Sunday seemed to go on forever and when I did

bump into someone it was a neighbour who offered 'shame about the result?' *'Shame about the result?' It was a disaster – for today, tomorrow and the next day – is what I wanted to shout back at him!*

Instead I weakly offered a 'yes' and asked Max if he fancied an ice cream at home to try to make this sad, lonely feeling go away.

So off we went into the kitchen and on went the telly. Max – three years old and in his red Wales football shirt – takes his place in his chair at the kitchen table and out comes a Fab from the freezer. He tucks in. Wales are playing Croatia – it's live on TV.

'Who do we want to win, Dad?' says my innocent, sweet young football supporter, who's falling more in love with the game on a day-by-day basis. (He's a decent keeper actually!) 'Yellows or red and whites?'

Wales are in yellow. They've changed strip and it looks terrible.

'Wales, son. The yellows,' I reply, like a man with the weight of the world on his shoulders. 'They're losing,' I add.

'Like the Bluebirds?' he asks, and licks the bits off the top of his ice-cold Fab and smiles.

'Yes, son,' I sigh. 'Like the Bluebirds.'

That's football eh?

<u>JORDAN 1 WALES 0</u>

'Up goes the hand…the punch … if ever there was one.'
(Archie MacPherson, BBC commentator, Anfield, 1977)

A hand? That's all. A hand. His bent right arm goes up in the air into the dark Liverpool night. Thousands watch. Some can't look. No. Please tell me no. Dark blue. Dark blue with a little white piping. Blue. Dark blue. Of course it was a Scottish hand. The hand of Joe Jordan. The arm! The dark blue arm. You get used to this as a Wales sports fan. The disappointment. The sick, gut-wrenching feeling that will become so familiar at Wembley Stadium. The churn that tells you you're not going to the World Cup. That feeling when you're told you're not going to the party. No son, that's for us. You can't come to the top table. Never.

Argentina 1978? Ticker tape and Mario Kempes? You won't be seeing that. That's for Ally MacLeod's Tartan Army. Not for you, Welsh boy. Simple as. Ticker tape? In a flash, my country had kissed goodbye to taking on the beauty of the white and pale blue-striped pin-up players of Argentina. Mario Kempes, the Argentina striker, César Luis Menotti, the man who would be king, and the throbbing cauldron of the Estadio Monumental – all gone. Finished in a flash. Scotland fans go crazy as Don Masson scores a penalty. They go even crazier when Kenny Dalglish – King Kenny – scores the second to make it Wales 0-2 Scotland. Funny how everyone knows about Diego Maradona's 'Hand of God' in 1986 at the World Cup. Yet not many people talk about the Joe Jordan handball at Anfield in 1977, which ended Wales' World

Cup dreams. No-one talks about it. As if it never happened.

I can still see it now. People talk about Maradona's 'Hand Of God'. but this was just as bad. Maybe if Joe Jordan had handled against England there would have been more outrage. Maybe if Jordan hadn't won a penalty and duped the referee on that fateful night, Wales might have gone on to do well in the World Cup. Maybe John Toshack and Terry Yorath would have done better than the Tartan Army. Maybe Wales would have qualified for every World Cup and European Championship ever since. Maybe. Just maybe.

Watch it again. As I did as I wrote this. An arm. That's all. The arm went up in the air. Dark blue – not a red arm. Obvious. Clear. A big fist. A throw of the right arm. A kind of reverse hook – a hook that knocked us out.

Not that I knew at the time, mind you. I was only four years old.

In 1977, I was growing up in Ely, Cardiff, Wales, and far more interested in dressing up as Batman (and to prove it I've raided the family photos) ready to take on The Joker or some other crackpot.

When Joe Jordan was a coach at Tottenham Hotspur Football Club working alongside Harry Redknapp I rang the club to ask him about that night, about Scotland, and to ask him about the handball. But I was told he wasn't there. I left my number. That was a few years back. He never returned my call. Funny, that.

SATURDAYS

My fascination with the most beautiful game in the world started in 1982. The Joe Jordan/David Jones handball which saw Scotland beat Wales in 1977 at Anfield in a World Cup match really should have turned me off. But it didn't. You see, I was only a kid of four at that time, even though I remember my granddad – a lovely man, fondly known as Dick on the streets of Ely – watching the match that night on an old TV set in my grandparents' house. I grew up in a family that stopped for Five Nations rugby, the Grand National, Wimbledon and Test Match Cricket. It was a sports-mad house.

Saturday afternoons in Heol Carnau, Caerau, Cardiff - a long road of redbricked council houses on the west side of the city - were a highlight. My granddad watched sport all day and his day began with a sneaky look at the betting pages. He turned me into a 'start-at-the-back-of-the-paper fella'.

To this day, I'm still one of those. And, to be honest, if I hadn't seen the sporting papers at an early age, I doubt I would have gone into a career of presenting or reporting sport on TV. In fact, one of my early newspaper memories is of seeing *The Sun* on the morning after Steve Davis won his first World Snooker Championship in 1981. Little did I know then that I would end up working with Mr Davis at the Crucible, presenting BBC Sport's coverage of the UK Championship, Masters and World Championship.

So anyway, back to Saturday afternoons. Highlight of my week. And I can still chart my life through those afternoons. I could spend the next few pages describing the houses, the street, and the smell of my street as a kid. But I'll keep it brief and get on with the job. Saturday afternoons. The smell of great, home-cooked food – spaghetti bolognese – kids playing football in the sun (or rain, wind or snow), *Football Focus*, Saint and Greavsie, Peter O'Sullevan, David Coleman, the vidiprinter and the Cockle Man selling cockles, mussels and winkles.

Watching Wales on the TV playing at the Arms Park in the Five Nations. Hard men. Big men. Red scarves. Cans of stout. Salted nuts. Bill McLaren. My grampy with his *Daily Star* folded open at the racing pages, leg cocked over the armchair and occasional mild swearing at Peter O'Sullevan when finding out his 'bloody thing' came in seventh in the big race of the day. Then the Five Nations match on TV. Forget your fifty-inch flatscreen TV – this was an old thing. They don't make them like that anymore. Buttons to change the three channels. Hear that, kids? Three channels! Rugby on after the wrestling. No five live TV channels. No subscription. Just a TV licence and Frank Bough. Push buttons – 'get up off your backside and switch the telly over' buttons!

Sport on Saturday meant Dickie Davies on *World of Sport* on one side; Grandstand and Des Lynam on the other.

Saturday afternoons in February. Wet outside. An eight-year-old fascinated with his family shouting at the TV and at Wales. Probably the first rugby union international I can remember is Wales v France. They loved the French in my house. Serge Blanco. Legend. Losing to France didn't matter. Losing to England, however …

But despite the affection for rugby, it was football that we all grew to love and the sport that brought us together. Probably because of the effect the game had on me. I slept

6

football. Ate it. Breathed it. Lived it. Played it. Pretty much like Max does now.

I wrote about it when I was in junior school. Seriously. Match reports when I was just eight. When I was in the second year of Cwrt yr Ala Junior School in 1982, I used to sit near a window in the classroom (a makeshift cabin on a soggy, tired Welsh football pitch) but my love of sport got me into a spot of bother. My Monday morning English lessons with Mrs Salway usually ended up with us writing about something that had happened to us over the weekend. Most kids went to the beach, went swimming, went to the library. I went to the football. And one day Mrs Salway wrote in red pen beneath my story about Godfrey Ingram* joining Cardif City (see below for a Cardiff City history lesson if you don't know who Godfrey is):

'Jason, I do wish you would write about something other than football on a Monday morning.'

You see, something amazing happened to me in 1982. Yes, I started big school, but I also saw Wales v England! Yes – a Wales v England football match! My first big match.

*Godfrey Ingram joined Cardiff City from the San Jose Earthquakes in 1982 for a club record fee of around £200,000. He is genuinely considered to be one of the strangest signings for Cardiff City. And trust me, there have been lots of signing antics at that football club. He played eleven times. He scored two goals.

WALES v ENGLAND 1982

It was on the 27th April 1982 that I went to my first ever football match. And no ordinary match. It was Ninian Park on a warm April evening where, at the age of eight, I was introduced to international football. It was a game in the now-defunct Home Championship – the big one for all the fans from Wales and England. Hoddle, Mariner and Morley were bound for Espana 1982. Naranjita, the Spanish mascot, was once again ready to welcome an England team to a World Cup. They missed out on Argentina 1978 but were back for 1982. And they came to Cardiff to warm up and beat Wales. It was all a bit weird as I knew more about the England team than any of the Wales players. Viv Anderson was one of the first players that I had in my Panini sticker collection and I suppose he could well pass as my first football 'hero'. For an eight-year-old boy, on his first ever visit to a live football match, seeing such a player actually playing football before his very eyes was a dream come true. Ninian Park was where my dream to be part of sport began.

THE 1982 WORLD CUP

'Zico's my cousin!' said my next door neighbour as we kicked the Adidas Tango around the street. Everyone wanted to be Zico. The Brazil team of the 1982 World Cup is still regarded as the best team never to have won the tournament. They were beaten by an Italian team, led by the goalkeeping captain Dino Zoff, who won the World Cup thanks to the goals of a then little-known striker called Paolo Rossi. His three goals sank Brazil in the quarter finals and every football fan in the world whose team wasn't at the tournament cried. I can still see Socrates' sweat-stained yellow shirt in the heat of Espanyol's Sarrià stadium. It was mid-afternoon on the 5th July 1982 and the whole world tuned into perhaps the greatest match in FIFA World Cup history. Not even Falcao's veins and biceps could push Brazil through to the semi-finals (if you're from the YouTube generation, google 'Brazil v Italy 1982' and you will not be disappointed).

Rossi destroyed them with three sniping striker's goals and I was falling deeper in love with football and sport. Italy went on to beat Poland 2-0 in the semi-finals then beat West Germany 3-1 in the final with goals from Paolo Rossi at fifty-seven minutes, Marco Tardelli at sixty-nine and Alessandro Altobelli with nine minutes remaining. Paul Breitner scored the consolation goal.

Meanwhile England, the team I'd watched from the Ninian Park 'Bob Bank', back in April, had gone out of the tournament.

BRAZIL

A year after the World Cup, my mates at school were all talking about 'the match' that their dads were going to take them to on Sunday. It was June, and my mum and dad had decided to take us on holiday. We had great holidays. No cheap flights back then. No all-inclusive holidays in the sun. Just a caravan on the south coast, or Cornwall. This year, it was to be Weymouth. Many happy days were usually spent on the beach or on the grass in the sunshine outside the van playing football – but this year I was gutted that we were going away. All the class talked about was the Wales v Brazil friendly at Ninian on Sunday. Brazil! Socrates!

A nine-year-old football fanatic, I'd cried when the yellow shirts trudged off that field in Barcelona a year ago. Now I had the chance to see live those spectacular athletes whose glorious failure had won the hearts of the world (apart from those living in Rio de Janeiro or Salvador!).

'Mum, it's Brazil! The team we watched in the World Cup! They're playing in Cardiff. Mum! Brazil!' I ran up the path screaming at the top of my voice.

'When? When is it, Jas?' said my mum

'The teacher says next week.'

It was, in fact, Sunday 12th June 1983 – and we were going on holiday on Saturday 11th June 1983.

'We're in Weymouth.'

'Weymouth? Weymouth, when Socrates is playing a few miles down the road?'

As much as I wanted to go on holiday, that weekend was one of the most miserable I've ever spent. It was a

Sunday kick off. Ninian Park was packed to the rafters and it was live on ITV. Our caravan was equipped with a TV. A black and white one. So – the biggest football day of my life so far was ruined by a family holiday to an English town on the south coast and a black and white TV!

I even think we had to put a metal coat hanger into the back of the telly just to get a decent picture. All my mates were at the game and all I could do was look on jealously as Socrates walked up to the centre circle to shake hands with the Wales players.

So imagine what that caravan was like when Brian Flynn scored a diving header at the far post in front of the Canton Stand, where I'd sat loads of times the season before watching Cardiff City win promotion. Great – but so frustrating. I'd notched up games against Cambridge United, Portsmouth, Newport County and Orient but missed Carlos Alberto, Socrates and Eder! Wales drew 1-1. Mum and Dad, I've never told you this – in fact it's taken me thirty-one years – but I never wanted to go on that holiday.

FA CUP FINAL

I loved FA Cup finals on TV. The first one for me was the Tottenham Hotspur v Manchester City replay in 1981. You know, the Ricky Villa one. Then Spurs v QPR and the replay. Then Manchester United v Brighton and Hove Albion – the Saturday game and the Wednesday replay. Ray Wilkins' curler for United in the 2-2 draw in 1983 is still one of my favourite Wembley goals.

I listened to football whenever I could, too. Ian Rush, Kevin Ratcliffe and Mark Hughes taking on England at Wembley. Cup semi-finals. Cup Finals. Would there be anything better in the world than being paid to watch football, I wondered? To this day Peter Jones is one of my all-time broadcasting heroes.

I'll never forget being in a car after going to a wedding on FA Cup Final day in 1985 and begging my dad to have the match on the radio. I was eleven. Manchester United v Everton had gone into extra time. We'd sneaked out of the reception and seen Kevin Moran become the first man ever to have been sent off in a Cup Final. Two kids aged eleven and six nipping into a bar full of big men watching the match on a big screen. Mum was worried. Where were we? But off we went to see if Neville Southall, Pat van den Hauwe and Kevin Ratcliffe – our Welsh boys – could beat a United side with Mark Hughes (more about him later). We wanted Everton to win on the grounds that there were more Welsh boys in the team.

Remember, these were days before Radio 5 Live and Sports Extra, so all commentaries were on Radio 2. *Sports Report* was on the same station.

'Da, da, da, da, da, da, da, du, da, da, da, da duh!' The theme tune to *Sports Report*! Peter Jones was an amazing commentator. He famously broadcast 'Whiteside's galloping down the right for Manchester United, curls it in, oh my word! Norman Whiteside! Could have won the cup for Manchester United!'

Even though we didn't want Ron Atkinson's team to win, I vividly remember Jones' commentary raising the hairs on my neck so that they tickled against my grey velvet wedding-special tank top. Whenever I hear the clip, it brings tears to my eyes. That is the mark of a special broadcaster. He died in 1990 while commentating at the Boat Race. One of the Great British Radio voices. He never knew me. But I knew him. He taught me so much about football and radio. And when I made my first appearance on BBC Radio 5 Live in 2009, Peter Jones, the voice, the FA Cup Final and my little radio in the shape of a panda came flooding back to me. I could almost have cried. That's the magic of sport and broadcasting.

A LOVE OF SPORT

I'd always wanted to work in sport. Obviously I'd like to have been a player, but as the assistant manager at Victoria Park Football Club once told me, as I was about to kick off against Wiggins Teape FC under 16s in a pre-season friendly as a centre forward:

'See, son, you'll always probably be a stone too heavy for football.'

In 1990, I won the Most Improved Player of the Year Award. I wanted to shove the manager's words down his throat. So, following a move into centre midfield and a diet and a few stunning strikes from the edge of the eighteen-yard box, I proved that I could mix it with some decent footballers on the parks of Cardiff. But it was clear from a very early age that my dream of playing for Wales would never be fulfilled. Never mind.

There was one other option, of course, which was getting as close as I could to the game by taking up a career in journalism. I'd always been fascinated by the glitzy and glamorous work of television and radio. I started writing for my school newspaper when I was thirteen. Sport was in my blood. I was born with a cricket bat in my hand. With a dad originally from Pakistan, it was inevitable that I'd play cricket – but I wasn't in love with it. Sure, I adored Mohsin Khan, Imran Khan and Abdul Qadir. Javed Miandad is still one of my top five favourite sportsmen of all time. The Pakistan team of the early 1980s really was a pleasure to watch.

We once went on a family trip to London on the train to see my dad's uncle, who lived in the centre of town in quite a nice pad, from what I can remember. And just a stone's throw away from Lord's. When we got there, like most Pakistanis living in the UK, he was glued to the BBC's Test Match coverage. I loved the TV coverage and as a Cardiff boy also used to go to watch Glamorgan at Sophia Gardens, spending memorable days watching Matt Maynard, Steve James, Steve Watkin and Waqar Younis. Glamorgan have a great tradition of taking on overseas players, and I came very close to choosing one of them for my Welsh sporting heroes. I played a bit of cricket and was quite a good batsman and bowler (when I could run) and I still play now – even at the grand old age of forty-one! Perhaps I've even played against you!

Choosing my seven top sports stars is an almost impossible task. There are so many great sportsmen and women who don't make my list. But what I have drawn up is my Magnificent Seven. My heroes played their sports hard. They are Welsh. They make us proud. They were (in some cases, still are) formidable on the football pitch, the rugby pitch, the track and in the boxing ring - and I had the pleasure of working with them all. They are my sporting heroes, and possibly yours too!

MARK HUGHES

I'll let you into a little secret. Even though I was born in Cardiff, my first ever football kit was the Liverpool European Cup winners' shirt of 1984. You know the one: the Crown Paints red with a pinstripe. They were tight shirts, too. Way too tight for a chubby eleven-year-old kicking a ball around in his grandparents' back yard. In fact, somewhere in the family archives, there's a film of me running around in the red shirt with a blue vest hanging out of the back. Not many people have seen that video, so don't even ask! It is slightly embarrassing.

Liverpool Football Club – the mighty LFC – were the dominant force in British football at that time. The LFC team of Bruce Grobbelaar, Kenny Dalglish and Ian Rush was – arguably - the greatest British football team to play in the twentieth century. Sir Alex Ferguson and Manchester United fans will disagree! So really I should be sitting here telling you that the player I loved most in the 1980s was Welshman Ian Rush. That would make perfect sense. Rush was Wales' all-time record goalscorer - the man who scored perhaps the most important goal in Welsh football, beating the then World Champions Germany in 1991 at the old Cardiff Arms Park.

I was there that night and I still remember what a brilliant goal it was when Rush sprinted away from Guido Buchwald and fired into the German net. Then there's Rush's performance in 1986 in the FA Cup Final when he rounded Bobby Mimms to land The Double for LFC – meaning Kevin Ratcliffe and Gary Lineker left Wembley Stadium empty-handed. Still, to this day, that FA Cup

Final – with John Motson's BBC TV commentary – is one of my favourite footballing memories from the old Wembley Stadium.

But this isn't about Ian Rush. This is about a boy from Ruabon in North Wales. This is not my memory of the boy from St Asaph who became a Liverpool legend. You're probably feeling that this is quite a strange story. How can a very young Liverpool supporter be choosing a Manchester United legend as one of his sporting heroes? But there is nothing strange about this. Forget great sporting rivalries, forget the great footballing rivals of Liverpool and Manchester United. When you're Welsh you love seeing Welshmen doing very well and Mark Hughes was the best.

Mark Hughes was the epitome of British football in the 1980s, a tough tackler, scorer of fine goals, and leading the Manchester United line. Don't forget he also played for the biggest clubs in Europe: Barcelona and Bayern Munich.

But it's his time with Wales as a player and a manager which squeezed him into my list of the greatest sporting heroes. Mark was born in North Wales in 1963. So when I first started watching football in 1982, I saw the young Mark developing into a fine international footballer - and in 2002 into a very good football manager. In fact, I was there when the Football Association of Wales announced that he was the new manager of Wales, taking over from Bobby Gould. And I was lucky enough to interview Hughes when his club at the time, Southampton, allowed him to become a part-time player/manager.

There are a number of amazing moments in Hughes' career which I was lucky to see. The first was in April in 1985 at the Racecourse in Wrexham, playing Spain in a World Cup qualifier. Once again Wales would lose out on a World Cup place in Mexico at the finals in 1986 but we'll come to that later. Many of you may never have seen Hughes unbelievable overhead kick (though I'm told it's available on YouTube). However, some of you older readers will remember this one.

Whichever, I can guide you through it. I'm going to describe it for you as if I'm a TV commentator ... (Picks up microphone)

'Robbie James floats over a free-kick into the Spain box, it's headed clear by the Spanish defence but only as far as Hughes on the eighteen-yard box. Hughes. Goes up – Hughes! ... Hughes scores for Wales! Oh my word! That is unbelievable. Unbelievable. What a strike from the Manchester United man! Wales' players mob him – they're all over him - they can't believe it either. The Racecourse has erupted. The greatest goal I have ever seen. The keeper had no chance. A bicycle kick from the penalty area. I repeat – a bicycle kick from the penalty area. What. A. Goal.'

Now you try it. Come on, I'm sure you've commentated on a match in the garden or the street. I did. And that's probably why I'm doing what I do now on TV! Wales went on to win the match 3-0 but sadly missed out on qualification to the FIFA World Cup in Mexico because of a dodgy penalty decision at Ninian Park. Scotland were the victors in that one – even though Mark scored a great goal early on in that match, too.

So where did it all go right for the Welshman? Well, it began in March 1978 when he signed schoolboy forms for Manchester United as a fourteen-year-old. In 1980, Mark signed professional terms with United, then made his debut on the 30th November 1983 against Oxford United in the League Cup. He scored in that game - and went on to score a further 162 goals in 467 matches. Sir Alex

Ferguson – who knows a thing or two about football – once said Hughes was the 'the best big-game player I have ever known'. He was tenacious, tough-tackling, brave, technically brilliant and, as I've described, a scorer of absolutely stonking goals. If he was to be playing now I have no doubt he would be an £80-million player. He was that good. And he was Welsh – thank God!

Hughes also scored on his debut for Wales – a 1-0 win over England in the final Home Championship match against the English. A fine way to start his international career. He went on to score sixteen goals in seventy-two matches for the boys in red.

A goal often omitted in Mark's best came on the 9th September 1987, when he scored at Ninian Park against the mighty Denmark side including Michael Laudrup and Preben Elkjaer. There is no doubt that, at this time, there was only one player I wanted to be, only one shirt I wanted to be in. I got soaking wet standing on the Bob Bank that night – but as a thirteen-year-old lad the only shirt I wanted was the number 10 Wales Hummel jersey. Sadly, the only thing I got that night was a match programme and not Mark Hughes' shirt. Yet again, Mark would miss out on another major finals – the Euro '88 tournament – won, of course, by the great Ruud Gullit-inspired Netherlands team. But when you watch that goal again you realise just how brave he was. A Robbie James header across the face of the goal, Andy Jones against the bar – and a flying header from Hughes to send the fans in the Canton stand into a frenzy!

I would have to wait twelve years to meet my hero.

On the 5th August 1999, I was sent to Southampton and it is days like these which make me absolutely love my job. I was a reporter with BBC *Wales Today* and covered the Sports News and by now, having played for United,

Barcelona, Bayern Munich and Chelsea, Mark was appointed as Wales' new football manager. He would still play for Southampton but would coach Wales on a part-time basis. And Mark brought the good times back to Welsh football.

In fact he gave me a bit of an exclusive, saying he was considering hanging up his international boots in order to concentrate on making the Wales job his own. Remember, Wales had been awful under Bobby Gould.

Mark Hughes was speaking for the first time since his appointment as caretaker manager. I remember him clearly saying that he was completely focussed and committed to reviving the fortunes of Welsh football. And, with so many great players at his disposal, like Gary Speed, Ryan Giggs and Craig Bellamy, we were looking good for qualification for Portugal 2004. But you know how that story ends, don't you? Yes – we missed out again.

In a luxurious Southampton hotel, Mark Hughes described his appointment as successor to Bobby Gould as 'an immensely proud' moment. I remember thinking at the timethat the Football Association of Wales (for once) had got this right. They'd turned to one of Welsh football's most respected figures. He knew exactly what was ahead of him.

The job, however, was the end of his international playing career. He so wanted the post on a permanent basis - he'd almost made his mind up to ditch his new player-manager tag.

He got off to a great start– with Ryan Giggs getting the winner in a qualifier in Belarus – but Wales failed to qualify for 2002 World Cup after winning just two of their last twelve games. By now, Mark (known as Sparky) was the full-time boss and was lucky to survive after such a poor run. But we stood by him. The FAW stood by him. It was almost inevitable that it would take time. But you could see that Wales were growing as a team and, after wins over Finland, Azerbaijan (twice) and Italy, it looked as if we were on our way to Portugal 2004. In fact, *that* night in the Millennium Stadium will never be forgotten. Goals from Craig Bellamy and Simon Davies gave Wales a 2-1 European Championship qualifying win against Italy in front of 72,000 screaming mad Welsh fans! Wales were suddenly hard to beat. Solid, hard-working and tenacious – just like the old gaffer! But then came disaster. In 2003, Wales slipped from top spot in the qualifying group after defeats by Serbia and Italy and were then beaten in the play-offs by Russia. You almost knew that the Mark Hughes love affair with Wales was nearing its end. I spoke to Mark backstage at the BBC Cymru Wales Sports Personality of the Year Awards in Cardiff. He said Wales had simply run out of steam by the end of the campaign.

It was a wonderful time following Wales back then. Hughes had put pride back into the shirt after the disaster of the Bobby Gould era. Wales were playing in front of sell-out crowds in Cardiff. Teams came to Wales knowing they were in for a tough game. We even went to Italy thinking we could win. But we were spanked 4-0 in the San Siro. It's tough following Welsh sport, isn't it? After draws against Azerbaijan, Northern Ireland (the Robbie Savage fight club match) and defeats to England (at, of all places, Manchester United's Old Trafford) and Poland in the opening four matches of the FIFA World Cup 2006 qualifiers, another campaign was over and so too was Mark Hughes' reign as Wales boss.

He left to manage Blackburn Rovers and I remember almost being in tears seeing him leave and the much-loved Gary Speed deciding to call it a day after a 3-2 defeat to Poland in Cardiff. Hughes had been a great servant to

Wales as a player. He didn't make a World Cup or a European Championship as a player but as a manager almost took us to a major finals for the first time since 1958. He made us believe. A proud Welshman and my favourite footballer of all time. Thanks Sparky for the memories.

JOE CALZAGHE

I've thought about this one long and hard. Do I tell you the story of how Joe went from Newbridge to the King of the World or do I just tell you my Joe Calzaghe-Al Pacino-Jason Mohammad-Las Vegas-Planet Hollywood story from 2008?

Let's get Joe Calzaghe's phenomenal record out of the way, then. Probably Wales' greatest ever sportsman. He was undefeated world super-middleweight and light-heavyweight boxing champion when he announced his retirement in February 2009.

Calzaghe was thirty-six at the time and reigned as a world champion for more than eleven years. It was an incredible run – he was saying farewell to the ring with a glittering record of forty-six wins from forty-six fights.

At the time he said it was a difficult decision but I believed that the time was right. It was a brilliant career, taking in great nights in Wales, England and the United States of America. The man who held the WBO, WBA, WBC and IBF super-middleweight belts during his sixteen-year professional career had finally cracked the US game the year before. We talked about America the first time I met him. Always smiling after news conferences, Calzaghe was a joy to be with. Even though he was a World Champ, Joe always had time for local journalists and I remember just how charming, generous and warm he was when I interviewed him for the very first time.

We met at the Cardiff International Arena in June 1999 – a few days before his clash with Australian Rick

Thornberry. We had coffee as the cameraman set up the chairs and lights for the interview. There is, inevitably, a sense of nervousness when you meet a sports star for the very first time. But I always think that they are more nervous than me. I'm used to the lights and the cameras – whereas I'd be a wreck if I was walking out in front of a baying mob into a ring about to get hammered in twelve three-minute rounds of top-class boxing. (Boxing is the only sport I've never, ever tried!)

It was the countdown to the world-title fight against the man from Australia - with the world champion predicting a quick finish. There was no sign of nerves at all from Joe. Softly spoken, he looked amazingly fit, and a man comfortable with his talent and his star status.

Calzaghe was to defend his WBO Super-Middleweight Championship at the CIA on the Saturday night, knowing that an impressive performance would lead to a big-money date in America later that year. (Little did Joe know he'd have to wait until 2008 for *that fight* with American legend Bernard Hopkins.)

What impressed me most in our TV interview was that Joe Calzaghe pulled no punches, saying he would win inside three rounds. It's all part of the boxing world – the home fighter says he's going to destroy the underdog. Remember that at this time, a few days before his fourth successful world title defence, lots of sportswriters had publicly criticised the quality of fighters Calzaghe had come up against.

Thornberry was also relatively unknown, and that may well have been the reason why Calzaghe hadn't landed a big money deal. But he was winning – and that was the whole point. Calzaghe was a winner. He beat Thornberry…and the rest – including a stunning fight with Jeff Lacy in 2006 and Mikkel Kessler in front of fifty thousand fans at the Millennium Stadium.

Then came the real heavyweight clash in 2008. Joe versus Bernard Hopkins. Joe's moment in the international spotlight had arrived. I, like other journalists, had described this as 'The fight of the decade!' I absolutely loved following Joe's career while working for BBC Wales. But my assignment to Las Vegas is still my favourite Welsh sport moment of all time. Who would not want to be in Las Vegas – Sin City – for one of the biggest Welsh bouts ever?

But let's put aside the boxing for a moment, because before the fight with Hopkins, there was a real heavyweight clash *outside* the ring.

Two greats of boxing and cinema clashed at a movie premiere in Las Vegas. In the red corner was Newbridge's Joe Calzaghe, and in the blue corner Hollywood's Al Pacino! It was a brilliant moment, no doubt, for Joe and his family – but also for me. I was out there following Joe's every move working for BBC Sport Wales and we got wind of a film premiere in the Planet Hollywood hotel in which we were staying.

We managed to blag some tickets and I found myself on the red carpet talking to the Godfather himself – the one and only Mr Al Pacino. Instead of reporting on the boxing, suddenly I found myself filming an exclusive interview with a Hollywood legend.

The man famous for winning an Oscar for *Scent of a Woman* and one of my favourite movies, *Carlito's Way*, told me how much he admired Calzaghe. Pacino said watching Calzaghe fight 'was almost like acting' and that he was a huge fan of the sport – like many other big stars from the world of entertainment.

Even to this day, I get a bit emotional talking about the moment I met one of my great acting heroes when covering an event with one of my great sporting heroes! Especially when you consider how we got the interview in the first place. When Al Pacino walked along the red carpet, I shouted 'Hey Al!' And he shouted back 'hey Jason!' Can you believe it? Tony Montana, Michael Corleone – Al Pacino knew my name! This was one to tell the grandchildren and readers of my next book (this one of course!) How do you top that? So – on camera – we had a chat about boxing and he was so charming and lovely.

He's one of my favourite A-list movie actors. I was watching some of the other correspondents and they were putting their arms around him for a piece to camera so I thought I'd do the same. After all, you only get one chance to do something like that in a lifetime.

The biggest stars I'd met up to that point were Tom Jones, Shirley Bassey and George Best. But this meeting with Pacino would top it all off. Amazing.

Oh, and Calzaghe won. Well done, Joe.

IEUAN EVANS

My next legend, ladies and gentlemen, is the one and only Ieuan Evans – star of rugby field and of TV.

This guy has a very special place in my heart. Not only did he give us so many great moments on the rugby field in the red of his beloved Llanelli, Wales and British and Irish Lions, but this fella is also one mean TV pundit. My first big TV show was the BBC Wales results show *Wales on Saturday* and we'd feature a combination of sports on the show, mostly football or rugby and package them up with insight and banter, from two legends, Leighton James – the former Wales footballer – and Ieuan. We had fab times in Studio C2 at Broadcasting House, Llandaff. Evans was quick-witted, intelligent (though he owes me a fiver for calling him that!) and brilliant at knowing when I needed him to fill in on TV for a few minutes. In fact, if you know someone at BBC Wales, you may even find the moment when my live satellite link went down from Northern Ireland v Wales, and 'Ieus', as we used to call him, had to read autocue! Think Ron Burgundy in *Anchorman* – but not as good! Hilarious. And one of the nicest men you're ever going to meet in sport. Unless, that is, you're playing football against him.

Like many great sportsmen, Ieuan Cennydd Evans is good at most sports. In the 1980s he came to Caerau RFC (where I was a handy baseball backstop) to play a summer baseball fixture – and he was decent with the bat. I remember joining the queues of Ely kids trying to get his autograph. Many, many years later, I.C. Evans would join the BBC Wales Sport team for a game of five-a-side football at Gôl in Leckwith. One rainy afternoon, Evans turned up in head-to-toe sponsored sports gear looking the real deal whilst the rest of us just threw on any old kit we could find. Sports stars, even when they retire, still get boxes of stuff delivered to their homes. OK, it doesn't fit as snugly as it did when they trained every day playing top-class sport, but it still looks great. Much better than us anyway, who looked like a really bad Sunday League team.

I went for a ball midway through the game, moving out wide on my right foot, running full speed, the five-a-side goal in my sight, thinking: if I pulled the trigger now and hit the target surely I'll score – dodgy keeper in goal. But I could see a huge frame moving closer to my head and ribs … closing in on me … fast … time to shoot? Nope, I took another touch – and whack! Smash! A monster of a man crashes into my left shoulder with his right shoulder like a juggernaut! Bang! I hit the side of the pitch. In fact, I hit it so hard I could smell the paintwork – the fence is still shaking to this day! I got up, aching with pain, and standing over me was one I.C. Evans – rugby legend – giggling...

'OK Evans – easy now – calm down, son!' I said.

He laughed. 'Well, now you have something to tell your mates in the pub!'

'What? You fouled me?' I replied.

'You've just been barged by a British and Irish Lion!' laughed Evans as he ran away to nail someone else!

If we'd had a ref, no doubt he'd have been walking. But as it was just a bit of five-a-side fun I built up my rage to get revenge on the player I'd idolised as a kid. But you know what? I couldn't catch him. He was too quick. We shook hands and laughed our heads off at the end of the match and, as we trudged off in the afternoon rain before heading back to the office, I thought to myself that this would make a great story when I wrote my memoirs. And here we are – many years later – looking back at the Welsh sports stars I've been lucky enough to interview and work alongside and I'm able to share my story with you. He's a great guy. One of the best.

Ieuan is regarded as one of the best rugby union wingers of all time. Ask any Welsh rugby fan for their favourite Evans moment, and I'm pretty certain they would mention the name Rory Underwood, the venue of Cardiff Arms Park, and the year 1993.

It was the 6th of February in the old Five Nations Championship and the all-conquering England team had rolled into Cardiff intent on smashing the Welsh and sealing an unprecedented third successive Grand Slam. They had won nine successive Championship matches, with Jeremy Guscott and captain Will Carling in sparkling form. Many of my pals say this is one of their greatest Welsh sporting moments. After all, it was Ieuan, it was Cardiff but, most importantly, it was against England. Evans himself described what happened that day in an interview he gave to the BBC sport website in January 2005.

He said that with the ball hoofed upfield by Emyr Lewis, he expected to chase 'forlornly' after the kick, as so often happens on the wing. He thought about asking Emyr why he hadn't passed to him when he realised, as he galloped up the field, that there was no one else there; he realised he had a chance. He beat Rory Underwood to the ball, kicked it on, and 'the roar of the crowd' took him the rest of the way. Not bad, having, by his own admission, barely touched the ball all the rest of the day.

He's being polite. When he talks about 'managing to get there just before Rory Underwood' – he's being Mr Nice again. Rory was sleeping and Ieuan took full advantage. As the great Bill McLaren BBC commentator said in his live match description:

'...up goes Ieuan Evans...Ieuan Evans is away...can the Welsh captain make it? He's going to do it. And it's a try for Wales! And the Welsh captain has scored his eighth try in his thirty-third international! Cardiff Arms Park is on its feet!'

Bill McLaren – simply the best.

Cardiff Arms Park was indeed on its feet. In fact, the place went nuts. The Millennium Stadium is a beautiful stadium – one of the best in the world – but believe me, younger readers, there was nothing better than the sound of a Cardiff Arms Park full of boozed-up fans about to witness a win over T.O.E. (The Old Enemy) .

Wales went on to win the match 10-9, hanging on to end England's Grand Slam dream! The perfect day.

Evans is also considered a legend for the Llanelli Scarlets, pulling on that famous red jersey 231 times, scoring 193 tries. He also led them during the 1996-7 season.

In 1997 he made the decision to leave his beloved Llanelli for Bath – and his impact was instant. They won the Heineken Cup in 1998.

As for Wales? Well, he made his first international appearance for Wales against France in Paris in 1987. And went on to win seventy-two caps for Wales, twenty-eight of them as captain, and scored thirty-three tries - at that time a record for Wales.

And as we know he was also so good that the selectors couldn't deny him a place on the plane to Australia, New Zealand and South Africa on the British and Irish Lions tours of 1989, 1993 and 1997. His four tries against the mighty All Blacks on that tour of 1993 made him the Lions' top try scorer. A true legend for club, country,

Lions and his BBC five-a-side team! (I forgive you Evans!)

Ieuan is now – and has been for many years – a top rugby pundit for Sky Sports. His love of rugby, his intelligence and his clear analysis make him one of the best in the TV business. We made him the broadcaster he is, of course! Our time on *Wales on Saturday* – from the office, to the makeup room, to the studio – will always be very special to me. Very few sports stars make the transition from pitch to TV or radio studio with such ease and professionalism. Ieuan had the ability and unique style to make him a TV star – speaking clearly and giving the viewer a sense of what was going on in the mind of the rugby internationals on the pitch.

One of the reasons why *Wales on Saturday* was so successful was the remarkable chemistry between me, Leighton and Ieuan. He was our leader when pulling on the red jersey of Wales and when he had an idea in the BBC Sport office, we would listen – largely because we respected him as a man and as a former captain of Wales. But you and I both know that the real reason we listened (and made his hot drinks all afternoon) was simply because we were afraid of being barged into a wall in the office.

Ieuan might already know this but I got my revenge on him with a cup of tea I made him in November 2008 before we went on air to discuss Cardiff Blues v Bath – I used out of date milk! Who's laughing now, Lion King?

BARONESS GREY-THOMPSON DBE

To be successful in any sport you need to have a good team: solid people around you with nerves of steel, as you and the others take on the best in the world. If you're in a team sport, you have to look out for each other in the heat of sporting battle. If you're involved in an individual sport, you will undoubtedly need a team in place to be around you to win titles, break world records and claim gold medals.

You may think this is a little strange, but to be a winner in the world of media, you also have to have a great team alongside you. In television, it's a golden rule. When you're in front of the TV camera, you are the one the man in Tesco will want to chat to if Wales have just had a stinker in the Millennium Stadium. If you're hosting a TV show, you will get stopped in the street for a selfie. It used to be an autograph, but times have changed since the arrival of the smartphone. I like it – I really do. But some members of the public take advantage of your generosity and think that, just because you are a familiar face, they can poke fun at you or, in the most extreme cases, verbally abuse you. Some may argue it is all part of the glamour of being a front man. I disagree. I'll never understand why someone would have ago at a TV presenter on a train journey home after a hard day at the office.

What I do know is that when you work in the media, you must have a solid team around you. So now, in my countdown of the greatest sportsmen and women I've had the pleasure of watching and working with, we reach a star, a Welsh sporting legend and an icon. Baroness Grey-

Thompson – I call her Tanni when we work together - has been an inspiration for millions of people around the world. Is there a tougher competitor in this list? Well, she's the only Dame, anyway. She's also a person I can safely say I have loved working with. Tanni is the most professional woman I have ever spent time with in a TV studio. We hosted a number of BBC Wales Sports Personality of the Year programmes together. From the first script meeting, through the rehearsals to the night of transmission, I pinched myself sometimes, realising that I was working with someone – actually standing next to – a Paralympian who has changed the game for disabled athletes and whose story is nothing short of inspirational.

Just before Christmas, as I prepared to head to Melbourne for the 2006 Commonwealth Games (plenty more about these amazing Games later) came a big announcement. Dame Tanni Grey-Thompson was to lead the Welsh team in Australia, becoming the first elite athlete with a disability to captain a national team.

I would get to know Tanni as Wales captain very well on that trip down under, interviewing her on the success of the team but also seeing her win the Team Wales Question of Sport Night that's traditionally held in the team hotel. And, of course, not only was she used to picking up medals on the track, but also very good at answering questions about all sports. A real winner!

That same year, after an amazing time at the Commonwealths, Tanni and I would co-present the BBC Cymru Wales Sports Personality of the Year Awards for the very first time. I'd been doing the gig since 2003, when Nicole Cooke won it – and indeed was host in 2004 in Cardiff's St David's Hall when a certain Tanni Grey-Thompson scooped the prize for the third and final time. She'd had a great year, winning two Gold medals in the

100 metres and 400 metres at the summer's Paralympics in Athens, taking her tally to eleven golds overall. Now, in 2006, she told me she was nervous as the director counted us into the show.

'Nervous? You?' I said.

'Yes, really nervous,' replied Tanni.

'You'll be amazing.'

And I was right. She was a natural in front of camera, conducting her interviews with charm, warmth and friendliness. The winner that night at the Celtic Manor Resort was Joe Calzaghe (another one of my heroes). And as we reflected on a job well done that evening of Sunday 3rd December 2006, I knew that Tanni and I would be friends forever and that we would *definitely* be doing the show together the next year. We were a solid team. That bond had been sealed when I was reporting on the glory of Team Wales' performance in Melbourne and, seriously, when you host a live, high-pressure show like the Sports Personality of the Year, you must have on-screen chemistry and the ability to look out for each other. Just a short 'you're doing great' can make the world of difference and, even though this was her first one, Tanni's little nods to me really improved my performance. She was bringing all that 'nous' from the track into the TV studio and, boy, did it help. Truthfully, I was the nervous one – not Tanni. She was faultless that night. Her performance was just like watching her win a gold medal on the track – perfectly planned, and executed like a true professional.

We went on to host a number of shows together at BBC Wales and I want to thank Tanni here and now for being so amazing and helpful on those big sporting nights. There are also very few sportsmen and women I've come across who talk about what I call 'normal stuff' like family, life, houses or shopping. But Tanni is one of those people. Despite all her sporting success and her political career, she is so down to earth, and that's why we love her so much. She would always find time in our very busy schedule to have tea and a chat about families and kids – and I loved that. And she hasn't told me off – yet! – for addressing her as Tanni when she is now a Dame!

She hasn't changed over the years. We met at the IPC Athletics Championships in Swansea recently and we nattered so much we almost missed our live slot on BBC Radio! The other things I love about Tanni are a) she always leaves her phone on and is happy to come on to my radio show and b) is amazing for a news line (typical journalist eh?). In August 2014 Baroness Grey-Thompson told me that, after the success of Glasgow 2014, Cardiff, Newport and Swansea should jointly bid for a Commonwealth Games in the future and would have the venues to host it. This is an exciting prospect. When she speaks, people listen. I certainly did!

RYAN GIGGS

Sunday 6th December 2009, Carrington, Manchester (Manchester United Football Club training ground). I'm waiting for Ryan Giggs. Yes – Ryan Giggs, the Wales and Manchester United legend. According to Sir Bobby Charlton – World Cup winner with England in 1966 – one of the greatest football players to have graced the beautiful game.

No one knows this at the time, but the reason I've travelled 182 miles on a cold Sunday morning with a BBC camera crew is because the Welshman has won the BBC Cymru Wales Sports Personality of the Year Award, pipping cyclist Geraint Thomas into second place. I'm nervous. Giggs is training on Monday night when the Award show takes place and it's broadcast live on television so we're about to film the presentation of his Award. I've met Ryan before – but for some reason now I'm nervous. Sweaty palms. Hot. The reason? It is not Giggs, but because the man presenting the famous old trophy is Sir Alex Ferguson!

Here he comes. Down the spiral staircase, into our room. He shakes the hands of the TV crew and smiles. Thank goodness for that! The Gaffer looks happy. Ultimately, the reason he's happy is because this is a special day for His Boy. He's awarding Giggs a trophy which proves that Wales, despite losing him, still loves the Welsh wizard. And I have to say, the ten minutes that Sir Alex gave me were ten of the best of my career so far. I'll tell you more about Sir Alex in a minute – but I need to remind you of just what an amazing 2008 and 2009 Giggs had.

Yes, 2009 was a momentous year for the Cardiff boy. At the age of thirty-six, he became the most decorated player in English football with a record eleventh Premier League winners' medal won in that year.

The year before, Giggs had won the 2008 UEFA Champions League after a 6-5 victory on penalties over Chelsea in Moscow. And of course the former Wales captain also celebrated winning his record tenth Premier League after scoring the goal that sealed the title for Manchester United at Wigan Athletic. By coming off the bench he also equalled Sir Bobby Charlton's appearance record of 758 matches for United. What an amazing achievement.

Very few players keep going when they reach their mid-thirties but Giggs was having a fantastic time in the autumn of his football career. True, giving up Welsh international football in 2007, after winning sixty-four caps and scoring twelve goals, helped prolong his playing career. In fact Sir Alex Ferguson – his manager, mentor and the man who stole Giggs' Welsh three feathers red hat to keep out the cold in Russia on Champions League nights – told me that Ryan's decision to leave the Wales set-up when he did was vital in order to keep playing for United and winning medals.

He also described Giggs as 'a God' during our ten-minute chat. This conversation came at a time when Sir Alex wasn't speaking to the BBC so it was something of a scoop when I rang the Editor at BBC Wales to tell him we had an exclusive with Sir Alex. (I'm still not too sure if Sir Alex knew that it was the BBC he was speaking to!) He told me that he thanked his lucky stars that he went after Ryan to offer him his first professional contract with Manchester United on Ryan's seventeenth birthday on the

29th November 1990. He also told me about the impact Giggs had within the club in attracting young players to United and that Giggs would undoubtedly go down as 'one of the greatest footballers of all time'.

Think about that relationship between Ryan and his manager. We talk too often about the memories of Giggs flying past defenders and scoring incredible goals and we forget about the dynamic between Fergie and his star man. What was so special about that relationship? It was almost like a father and son team. As I talked to Sir Alex that day, his eyes lit up when he spoke of Giggs, like a dad glowing about his son. His affection for Ryan was clear to see. He cared deeply about him as a man and, perhaps more important, appreciated Giggs for the role he'd played in the fantastic teams Fergie has moulded.

Lots of players leave Old Trafford and spill the beans on what really happened inside that dressing room (you know who they are and don't' need me to tell you) but surely this would never happen to these two. First, Giggs is still at Old Trafford as part of Louis van Gaal's coaching team and, second, the bond appears to be too strong. Third, Sir Alex is proud of the fact that no manager would ever again have a player for more than twenty years. One club. One man. One manager.

Some managers get sacked after day one of the new football season. Some players barely last a season in one shirt. Money has changed the game. What Giggs did, in staying at the football club for such a long time, will never be repeated. But one does wonder what would have happened had Giggs signed for Real Madrid, Inter Milan or Barcelona. Should he have gone? Maybe so. It's an interesting debate.

But this is not a chapter on the Scotsman – widely regarded as the greatest British manager of all time – this is about Giggs. Ryan was also very generous in his interview that day, thanking the people of Wales for the accolade after a fine footballing year. Sure, he'd left Wales after losing to the Czech Republic at the Millennium Stadium on the 2nd June 2007, but the public in Wales still couldn't resist voting him as their Sports Personality.

Just a few weeks later, he was crowned 2009 BBC Sports Personality of the Year, beating Formula 1 champion Jenson Button into second place, with world heptathlon champion (and soon to be 2012 London Olympic Champion) Jessica Ennis getting third prize. Giggs was visibly shocked to be named the first footballer to claim the prestigious trophy since England midfielder David Beckham in 2001, with Michael Owen (1998), Paul Gascoigne (1990) and Bobby Moore (1966) the only other football winners. Esteemed company indeed.

I was there when Giggs announced himself on the world stage. He made his debut against the giants of Germany in Nuremburg in 1991, coming on as a sub at the age of seventeen years, 321 days, to become the youngest player to appear for Wales, under the stewardship of Terry Yorath. Two years later, another World cup campaign would end in heartache when Paul Bodin missed a penalty against Romania and we had another summer in Trecco Bay and not at USA 1994. I'll never forget the night when Giggs, Gary Speed, Ian Rush and Neville Southall trudged off the pitch on a cold November night with another campaign gone, having been so close.

But the main reason why Yorath and co. had come so agonisingly close in the first place was because of Giggs. He'd had a brilliant campaign, which started with a stunning goal from a free kick against Belgium on his home debut. He went on to play a key role in Wales' team of 1993 and Yorath always said that Wales would have done better in the World Cup Finals at USA 1994 than they did in the qualifying group. Sadly, Wales would miss out on another major finals, after another major disappointment. Some years later Mario Balotelli would start using the phrase 'Why Always Me?' Well, Mario, we've been saying that all our lives: 'Why Always Us?'

I'll keep the detail in this part brief. We lost to Romania in November 1993 after Bodin missed a late penalty and the magnificent Gheorghe Hagi led his team to an unlikely 2-1 win at Cardiff Arms Park. It was all over for Giggs, all over for Yorath, who left his post, and all over for Wales. Shame. Wales had built a great team. The fans were on board and we had a new superstar in Ryan to line up alongside Ratcliffe, Hughes, Speed, Saunders and Rush. Some of the best players the world has ever seen have pulled on the mighty red jersey of Wales – yet the world never saw them at their peak on the global stage.

Many years later, I would meet Giggs at Cardiff Airport when Wales were on their way to Milan to take on the mighty Italy in the San Siro in September 2003. We'd beaten the Italians 2-1 on a memorable night in Cardiff in October 2002. What a famous night for Welsh football that was – but there was to be no repeat in Milan as they battered us 4-0. And yes – you've guessed it – we missed out on qualification for Euro 2004 by a whisker. Giggs – under the leadership of another player who made this list, Mark Hughes – would never play in a major finals for Wales. But he is still one of the greatest players to grace the game: elegant on the ball, fast, skilful, scorer of utterly beautiful goals, deadly at a set piece and a joy to watch. He would have lit up a World Cup or European Championship but, like too many of the Welsh, he didn't get there.

His achievements in British football will never be beaten. I doubt that we'll ever see another Ryan Giggs. Some say Gareth Bale will be a better player for Wales over time. Maybe. They are two very different footballers. If Bale gets anywhere near Giggs' record and qualifies for a major tournament with Wales, he will have had a stunning career. But one club, one manager, one dream? Never again. Giggs is unique.

When he announced his retirement from playing Giggs had made a club record of 963 appearances for United and played sixty-four times for Wales. He is the most decorated player in the English game, having won thirteen league titles, four FA Cups and two Champions Leagues, among thirty-four trophies. Giggs – we salute you. And you never know – he may guide Wales to the World Cup in Russia 2018? Watch this space.

Ryan Giggs made ordinary nights against Finland and Azerbaijan extraordinary. His free kick against Belgium is, for me, his best for Wales, (watch it on YouTube) and I'll never forget walking into the cold Westgate Street night afterwards, glowing inside, knowing a star had been born way back in 1993.

DAVID DAVIES

I didn't go to the Olympics in 2004 in Greece but I watched all the action unfold on my TV screen. And during these Games another Welsh sporting star was introduced to the world stage (and Olympic podium). But fast forward to March 2006 and I was in Australia, which was a country I had always wanted to visit. I was sent to cover the Commonwealth Games for BBC Wales News – although it got off to a slightly strange start in that we arrived days before the competition was due to start. So what was a TV crew meant to do apart from eat and get some much-needed sleep? Well, we spent our time thinking of things to do to entertain the audience back home.

So, when in Melbourne, do as all the tourists do. Imagine the look on the producer's face when I told him that he could have an item on my trip to the set of the Australian TV soap *Neighbours*! Yes! Get in! A dream come true! *Neighbours*!

We thought we'd pay Harold Bishop a visit. How many people can say they've had fish 'n' chips with Harold from *Neighbours*? Bu that's exactly what happened after he showed us around Ramsey Street for an item for *Wales Today*. We produced a film of our guided tour with Harold (played by Ian Smith) who also told me that Wales was one of his favourite countries. Now I know what you're thinking – he's just told us about his world exclusive with Sir Alex Ferguson and now he's telling us all about Harold Bishop? Shall we get on with the sport? I think we should!

On 15th March 2006, 4,500 athletes from seventy-one

countries walked into the world-famous Melbourne Cricket Ground for the opening of the Commonwealth Games. And a few days later Wales were making all the headlines after an incredible evening in the swimming pool.

I can still remember that amazing feeling of seeing David Davies of Barry and Wales romping home to swimming glory at the 2006 Melbourne Commonwealth Games. It is one of the best moments I've ever had covering Welsh sport. How many times would a correspondent be in Australia and see a Welshman beat the Aussies in their own backyard, at a sport they love so much?

David Davies was a bronze medallist in Athens at the summer Olympic Games of 2004. He famously told BBC TV commentator Sharron Davies to 'calm down' in his post-race interview after coming third behind Australia's Grant Hackett, who'd won gold and successfully defended his Olympic crown in a new Olympic record time of 14:43.40. American Larsen Jensen took the silver medal.

In 2000, Davies was just fifteen and swimming in the Welsh Open. But just six years later he collected the country's first gold medal in the pool for thirty-two years. The twenty-one-year-old from Barry cruised to victory in the 1500 metres freestyle.

It was a golden night. Davies prepared superbly for the Games and he swam brilliantly in the 1500 metres. He was so good that the Australian crowd (and they know a thing or two about swimming) cheered him on during his final lap. It was an unbelievable moment and, for me, one of the great Welsh sporting tales.

I didn't know David at all before this trip. But during it we worked together on our coverage and, since then, he has been a really great guy to know. I've had the pleasure of being with him at sporting charity events and even bumped into him at a few Cardiff City matches.

That night in Melbourne on the 23rd March 2006 was his chance to break Australian domination in the 1500 metres. Tickets for swimming's finals night had been snapped up weeks before the Games had even started -- and a noisy crowd inside the pool based at the Melbourne Sports and Aquatic Centre was introduced to a Welshman who would become the first non-Australian to win the most gruelling event in the pool since 1954.

He led from start to finish -- he was simply too good for the rest of the field. The two Australians, Craig Stevens and Travis Nederpelt, struggled to keep up with Davies – who swam amazingly well to finish twelve seconds ahead of his nearest rival, Canada's Andrew Hurd.

The fans were on their feet. I was up in the stands cheering for David. I had a tear in my eye as Davies crossed the line. The boy from Barry had made us feel unbelievably proud and given us an incredible start to the Games!

Australians are crazy about swimming and when Davies was given the gold medal what followed was just phenomenal. The reception he got in the pool emphasised just what an achievement this was. David had just won the most coveted title in the pool, beating Australians in Australia.

For the Welsh fans, including David's parents who were watching in the stands, this was a moment to savour. For the Australians, it was an embarrassment. It had been a shocking Commonwealth Games for the men in the pool. Without the injured Ian Thorpe and Grant Hackett, Australia's men won just one gold medal.

It would certainly have been a different race had Hackett been there – but we didn't care. Our main man had become the first swimmer from Wales to win a Commonwealth title since Patricia Bevan's 200 metres breaststroke gold in 1974.

Two years later, in Beijing, Davies added to Wales' best Olympics medal tally for eighty-eight years by winning silver in the 10 km open-water swim and he fulfilled his dream of competing in the London 2012 Olympic Games before announcing his retirement from the sport in the November of that year.

For me, swimming doesn't get the respect it deserves in Wales and beyond, largely because we are far too obsessed with cricket, rugby and, most of all, football. And that's a shame because there are many amazing competitors in swimming. How many footballers or rugby players would be on the training paddock at 5.30 a.m., home for some breakfast and protein shakes, and then back training again later in the day? Not many. But that's a normal day for a swimmer. They are right up there as some of the fittest athletes on the planet and that's why Mr David Davies deserves to be in my list of Welsh Sporting Heroes.

SAM WARBURTON

I've given this so much thought. I've never been able to tell people my favourite film or favourite music track around a dinner table. There are just too many to choose. If we're talking movies – then *Carlito's Way* (starring my mate Al Pacino) would be in there, obviously. But so too *Goodfellas* and *Toy Story 1,2* and *3*. As for music, I don't have a favourite record – I have records. Michael Jackson's 'Thriller' is right up there with the soundtrack to *Pulp Fiction* – alongside Deacon Blue's 'Raintown'.

The same for my Welsh sporting stars. How can I pick one? So, as you've seen - I've narrowed it down to seven. My magnificent seven. And so it ends with the man who wears the number seven on the back of his shirt.

I've decided to put a few rugby players into my list of all time stars simply because I absolutely love the thrill of an international match day. My granddad used to watch all the Five Nations games and even used to get me old rugby programmes from the old Cardiff Arms Park. I now have the pleasure and honour of hosting Six Nations matches for BBC TV Sport, working alongside some of the game's greats, including Sir Clive Woodward, Justin Marshall, Jeremy Guscott and Keith Wood.

The next player on my list is Sam Warburton. Sam was brought up in Rhiwbina, Cardiff, and went to the same school as one of the world's best footballers, Gareth Bale, and Olympic champion cyclist, Geraint Thomas. An incredible achievement for the school and for Cardiff. Will any other Welsh school ever be able to match that? One of the world's great rugby players, the most expensive footballer in the world, and a gutsy gold medallist?

But the reason I've got Sam in my chosen few is because he's the captain of Wales, a fantastic ambassador for his city and country, and also a great guy.

Sam played for Wales at all levels and made his debut for the senior team on 6th June 2009, versus the USA. It was clear from the outset that Warburton was not only going to be one of the best flankers on the planet but also a leader of men.

I was lucky enough to see Sam score his first try for Wales against Italy in the 2011 Six Nations tournament in Rome. I was hosting the BBC coverage just a few yards away from the try line which Wales were attacking as Sam scored a great try, with James Hook passing inside for Sam to touch down at the Stadio Flaminio. Wales went on to win 24-16.

Later that year, the news broke that Sam was to captain Wales for the biggest test of Warren Gatland's tenure as Wales coach, the Rugby World Cup 2011 in New Zealand. What followed was nothing short of dramatic. You know what's coming next – so in the classic TV presenter warning, if you don't want to know the score and read about the red card again, look away now!

Sam was growing into one of the most respected rugby players on the planet. I'll never forget, just before this World Cup, queuing with my wife and three children to get into Wagamama in Cardiff. In front of me, I saw a huge man in a bodywarmer and training gear tucking into a big bowl of noodles. It was Mr Warburton out with his family. Now this is the mark of the man. He saw me, and got up and made a point of coming over to say hello to my family. To me, he is the nicest man in Welsh sport. Imagine what it was like for those young rugby fans of mine to meet with Sam Warburton, rugby hero. There he was – about to lead his country into the World Cup but happy to pose for a photo and meet fans, eating like a normal guy. These days, sportsmen and women are kept away from the public. Not many of them are comfortable with being in the limelight. Not like the good old days when football managers, rugby players and cricket coaches would invite journalists from the local newspaper in for a chat to talk tactics and family life. The PR machine likes to control things nowadays and I think that's sad. Frank Burrows – a former Cardiff City manager – used to invite us into his office for a chat before doing any interviews on City's forthcoming matches. That was in 1997. I've never been in a manager's office since.

But Sam is a likeable and down-to-earth lad, which made what happened to him and Welsh rugby on that day in New Zealand even more upsetting. I came very close to skipping this part as I thought it would be too difficult to put into words how I felt that day, sitting at BBC Radio Wales, about to host a phone-in on Wales making the Rugby World Cup Final. Sadly, it was not to be. Imagine how tough that was – taking calls from heartbroken fans after Wales came so close to beating France in the semi-final and taking on the not-so-mighty-minus-Dan-Carter All Blacks.

The eyes of the world were on Eden Park in Auckland for this mouth-watering northern hemisphere clash between Wales and France. We'd blown Ireland away in the quarter-finals and I very nearly went to New Zealand to cover the semi-final. I was asked on the Monday morning before Saturday's semi-final if I had anything on that weekend.

Within the space of an hour I was told to 'get ready to be sent home to pack' and then told 'actually you won't be going'. That's the nature of broadcasting, TV and radio.

It's a real adrenaline rush. I was a bit sad I wasn't there. Even sadder come the final whistle.

I can remember going on live radio the day before to tell the listeners that there was 'one more sleep and *the* match will be here.' Wales were about to play only the second Rugby World Cup semi-final in our history.

Sixty-five thousand fans were expected to pack the Millennium Stadium to watch on giant screens. The French team had a habit of turning up for World Cups and had demolished England the weekend before and sent Martin Johnson's team home from the competition.

The match stats didn't look great. The two countries had met on eighty-eight occasions previously, with Wales leading the series 43-42, with three draws. Our record win in the series was a 47-5 success in 1909, while France boasted a best of 51-0 at Wembley in 1998.

The last drawn Test match between Wales and France produced a 16-16 scoreline in Cardiff thirty-seven years ago. Surely not the drama of a low scoring game? Please, no extra time? France had won nine of the last eleven Tests against Wales.

Wales was going World Cup crazy, reaching our first World Cup semi-final since 1987.

The Wales captain Sam Warburton and number eight Toby Faletau were starting their sixth successive World Cup games, the only players among the squad with one hundred percent appearance records. (I'm sure that horrendous training camp in Poland where the players were forced to endure freezing temperatures helped!)

Anyway – back to the game. Wales had walked out looking unbelievably fit and confident. Thousands of fans had packed the stadium. Pubs were full. Clubs were running out of beer early on this Saturday morning. Nerves. Never before had the whole of Europe – possibly the world (bar France) been cheering for Wales. Even the New Zealanders, I am sure, wanted the dream final of Wales v the hosts. England fans were cheering for Wales. I repeat, England fans were cheering for Wales. But it wasn't to be. Not this time.

Sam Warburton – our leader – our hero – the man who would bring the Webb Ellis Trophy home and change sport in Wales forever – was sent off for a tip tackle at the base of the line out. This is how BBC Sport reported the moment:

'The game then turned on a hugely controversial call from referee Alain Rolland. Warburton, so impressive throughout the tournament, lifted Vincent Clerc off his feet with a big hit and then turned him in the air, leaving the Frenchman crashing onto his back.'

Alain Rolland. Alain Rolland. Did you realise what you'd done? Yes, it probably was the correct decision. But in a World Cup semi-final? The TV pundits were sure that the referee has spoiled the match, spoiled the whole occasion. The camera cut to Warby. Devastated. Warren Gatland was sure the referee has halted his team's march to the final. In a post-match interview he said:

'We just feel like the destiny of the result was taken out of our hands with the red card.'

True. Wales were looking like world beaters. For the first time in my sports broadcasting career, I honestly thought Sam was going to bring the Cup home to Wales. After so much disappointment watching Welsh sport, there was momentum. Gatland had brought belief, pride, emotion to our national sport. We'd won a Grand Slam in 2008 in his first season in charge. The players were fit; the fans were on board. We were going places. Sadly, at lunchtime on that Saturday (because of the time difference) the only place we were going – was home.

Still, Wales put in a phenomenal performance – playing with fourteen men for sixty-one minutes and narrowly missing out on a place in the final. Yet again. So many near misses. James Hook and Stephen Jones both had chances. Mike Phillips – a warrior from West Wales – scored a sparkling try, but it was all in vain. We lost 9-8. France were into the final.

There would be tears in the Valleys again. From North to South, grown men wept into their pints of Brains SA. Face paint was smudged on the faces of those who'd skipped to the Millennium Stadium to see their team reach the final. Children cried. The whole of the UK wept as France danced the night away in Paris. Allez Les Bleus.

Thoughts turned to Sam – how would he cope? Would people blame him? Of course not. There was only one villain here.

I had the job of lifting the nation back home in Wales, hosting a special phone-in on BBC Radio Wales. I remember saying this live on air:

'So that's it - our Rugby World Cup dream is over. This morning on Twitter at 7 a.m. I wrote: 'fasten your seatbelts' - but I never, ever thought it would be the rollercoaster ride that we've all been through. Perhaps the most heartbreaking image I have ever seen in my thirteen years of sports reporting and presenting was Sam Warburton - Captain Fantastic - head in hands on the touchline after being sent off by Irish referee Alain Rolland after a dangerous tackle on Vincent Clerc.'

Needless to say the phone lines lit up. Sam wasn't to blame. The listeners made it abundantly clear who they believed was accountable for this failure.

New Zealand went on to win the final. But to this day I firmly believe Wales would have won the World Cup. We could have beaten that All Blacks side. We'll never know.

What we do know is that Sam Warburton bounced back. He put the disappointment of Eden Park behind him, got on with the job of leading his country to another Grand Slam (in 2012 – beating France!) and in a magnificent British and Irish Lions series win against Australia in 2013.

To get over the heartache of missing out on World Cup and to do it in such style, puts Sam in my list of Welsh sporting heroes. A true Wales star – on and off the pitch.

DEEP INTO ADDED TIME

I've gathered together these memories while riding on a bus in the Black Sea resort of Sochi, while lying on Ipanema Beach in Brazil (yes, you do get some down time when working at the World Cup) and while sitting in a hot, sweaty hotel room in Sheffield when taking a few minutes out from preparation for the World Championship Snooker at the famous Crucible Theatre.

2014 was an incredible year for sport. It was the year of the Winter Olympics, the FIFA World Cup and the Commonwealth Games – and I was there to watch all the drama unfold. From Lizzy Yarnold's extraordinary gold medal in the skeleton in Russia, to the chaos of Brazil's 7-1 humiliation against Germany in Belo Horizonte, to Geraint Thomas' unforgettable gold medal in the road race in Glasgow, 2014 was every TV presenter's dream – a dream which began – as you now know - when I was a little boy growing up in Cardiff.

As you've also probably gathered – I love Wales. I love Welsh sport. I love the Welsh sporting family. Some say that, even though I don't play top-class sport, I fly the flag for Wales when hosting coverage of these global events. If that's true, then I am so proud to have been given this chance to represent my country. Sadly, I wasn't good enough in my role as a tough-tackling footballer to win a place in the Welsh team. My energy levels used to sap when I found myself at the bottom of a ruck in the second row for my youth rugby union club side, Caerau Ely. Maybe reporting on TV from the side of the pitch is the next best thing. I'm certainly having the time of my life.

I've also been very lucky to meet some amazing people over the past fifteen years. It would be impossible for me to broadcast to the nation without the help of editors, producers, camera operators and the sound department (in fact everyone I've ever worked with!). Broadcasting is very much like playing a sport – the success of any show is down to hard work and teamwork. There is very little margin for error when you are working in live TV and, even after all these years, I still get a phenomenal buzz from it.

I watched so many stars in 2014 who could have made it into this book. Just for a bit of fun I want to rattle off a few of the amazing sports men and women I have worked with, interviewed or watched during the last twelve months. They could all make my global list of sporting heroes because we had such a great year of sport in Great Britain and around the world. Some of these names could easily have sneaked into the main part of the book because they're Welsh and, well, quite frankly superb.

First mention goes to Frankie Jones – the Welsh gymnast who won six medals at the Commonwealth Games in Glasgow. Then there's Gareth Bale – the Welsh footballer who won the Champions League with Real Madrid in his first season at the club. Next comes Geraint Thomas – Welsh cyclist, double Olympic Champion and a gold medallist at Glasgow 2014. Finally, golfer Jamie Donaldson, the thirty-eight-year-old from Pontypridd, who won the Ryder Cup for Team Europe at Gleneagles.

Those four Welsh stars really deserve a mention in this book because they have had heroic years for Wales and Welsh sport and have given us such pleasure. Frankie had so much time for her fans at the SSE Hydro. In the second week, even though she had won medals and become a household name, she still had time to pose for photographs, selfies and signed autographs. When I bumped into her with my own children, Lili, Max and Poppy, she enabled them to have photos taken with the entire gymnastics team and now they want to become the next Frankie Jones. (Well, actually Max wants to play for Wales and win the World Cup and play alongside Gareth Bale in his later years!)

Bale's Real Madrid CF team-mate, Cristiano Ronaldo, would also get on my 'alternative sporting heroes' list simply because of the pleasure I took in watching him at the Cardiff City stadium when he played for Real in the Super Cup Final, beating Sevilla CF. He is a genius: a one-off who has an ability to score the sort of goal that really should only be possible when playing FIFA 15!

Lionel Messi, too, would make my 'alternative' list. I was at the World Cup Final at Brazil's Maracanã between Germany and Argentina and seeing Messi in the flesh was another dream come true. Although he has not yet reached the heroic status of Diego Maradona, I have a huge amount of respect for everything Messi has achieved in football. He is another footballing genius – a player who makes it all look easy. On the eve of the World Cup Final at a swanky TV studio in Rio De Janeiro, when I interviewed Daniel Passarella – the captain of the world-famous 1978 Argentina team which won the FIFA World Cup in Buenos Aries (the World Cup which Wales were robbed from attending) – he confirmed that Messi 'needed to win the World Cup to reach the God-like status' of Maradona. Argentina lost to Germany and Messi looked a tired shadow of the player who had lit up La Liga the previous season. Still, what a huge thrill it was to see one of the greatest players ever on the greatest stage of all!

Finally, I have to put the great Usain Bolt on this 'alternative' list. I have been in hundreds of stadiums, arenas, tracks, boxing rings and swimming pools all over the world, but when the fastest man on the planet stepped out at Hampden Park on a rainy Saturday night in Glasgow, I almost cried. The reason? I am now passing on my love of sport to my children. Lili, Max and Poppy, who are now eleven, seven and five, have the same passion for sport that I had when I was their age. Their little eyes lit up when Usain lined up for the 4 x 100 metre relay on that Saturday night.

I still clearly remember the smell of freshly cooked pies and pasties as I made my way to Ninian Park for my first-ever football match. I remember the circles of smoke from the old men's pipes and cigarettes, the smell of ale and the glow of the floodlights lighting up the Cardiff April night. And I remember the vision of the green, hallowed turf as I climbed the small set of steps into the Grandstand. On that evening in April 1982, the only thing I cared about was football and sport. Thirty-two years later, my children talk sport around the dinner table and 'the night they saw Usain Bolt' has become a hallowed memory for them.

We often talk about a 'legacy' and ask if 'sport really matters'. I can tell you – it most certainly does. Within a week of my children returning to Cardiff, they had joined an athletics club in the hope of being Team GB's next big thing. The power of sport and of this kind of experience is immeasurable.

My Welsh Sporting Heroes certainly fired a passion in me. Ryan Giggs, Sam Warburton, David Davies, Ieuan Evans, Joe Calzaghe, Mark Hughes and Baroness Grey-Thompson were stars in their own sports. I want each and every one of them to know that they inspired me and one or two of them continue to inspire the next generation.

Wherever I go around the world, I carry a card with me. It's only a greeting card but on the front it carries a photograph of The Greatest Sportsman of All Time and his most famous saying. The same picture and quotation are framed on my wall at home. I like a quote and I use this for inspiration whenever times are tough. It's a phrase I've used many times in my career. I leave you with it:

'Champions aren't made in gyms. Champions are made from something they have deep inside them – a desire, a dream, a vision. They have to have the skill and the will. But the will must be stronger than the skill.' Muhammad Ali.

Quick Reads 2015

My Sporting Heroes – Jason Mohammad
Captain Courage – Gareth Thomas
Code Black: Winter of Storm Surfing – Tom
Anderson
Cwtch Me if You Can – Beth Reekles

Á

For more information about **Quick Reads**

and other **Accent Press** titles

please visit

www.accentpress.co.uk